MW01048027

EASTER

TO

PENTECOST

Weekly Bible Studies based upon the Approved
Lectionary readings for the Anglican Church

1

Index

Foreward

Bible study! What springs to mind? Words like, boring, tedious, always being told what the text means. Also being told what I should be believing, but never why! These are just the polite ones. Bible study groups always seem to be for just a small group of church goers. Those who have often nothing better to do in the evening, and just need an excuse for a "churchy" social meeting with their friends. Usually it will be one of Paul's letters that is chosen for study, as these often contain rules for the church that can be discussed and agreed with or not. The usual pattern seems to be to study a chapter a week, even if the subject matter strays over the chapter line, and are usually led by the vicar or someone similar, who knows all the "right answers", and can correct you if you think in an original way, or disagree with the status quo view.

This may sound cynical, but is a fair reflection of many of the bible study meetings I have attended over the last fifty years. This, though, is only true if the church had Bible study groups. Many churches seem think them unnecessary. Or have tried them but nobody attended, unless it is a lent course. It would appear that you go to Sunday school, get confirmed, and that is the end of the Church's Teaching, apart from the weekly sermon. These may be good or bad, but do you ever get to ask questions about bits of them, ask the vicar for a fuller explanation? Probably not!

The ones I have enjoyed have taken small chunks of the Gospels, rather than Paul, and have been open discussion, everybody free to say what they feel and think. This style I have tried to replicate in this short 8 week bible study course.

I have taken the set Lectionary Gospel readings for 2015, working from Easter Sunday to Pentecost. They are taken in their own right, and looked at as such. No Influence from Paul, or the Church or any official "understanding" I have simply taken the readings from John's gospel and looked at what Jesus has to say.

It was not what I expected!

Why not get together with a few friends and try to come at the Gospels with an open mind, bearing in mind three questions.

5

What is Jesus saying and to whom?
What did it mean to his listeners?
What does it mean to us today?

The last question is perhaps the most important, but I give no correct answers. Jesus speaks to each of us, and what it means to each of us is individual. Hopefully, this makes Bible study more inclusive, more personal, and hopefully more useful to each of us on our Christian journey,

Easter Day

The Resurrection

John Chapter 20 v 1-18 (+19-23)

Early on the first day of the week, while it was still dark, Mary Magdalene went to the tomb and saw that the stone had been removed from the entrance. So she came running to Simon Peter and the other disciple, the one Jesus loved, and said, "They have taken the Lord out of the tomb, and we don't know where they have put him!"

So Peter and the other disciple started for the tomb. Both were running, but the other disciple outran Peter and reached the tomb first. He bent over and looked in at the strips of linen lying there but did not go in. Then Simon Peter, who was behind him, arrived and went into the tomb. He saw the strips of linen lying there, as well as the burial cloth that had been around Jesus' head. The cloth was folded up by itself, separate from the linen. Finally the other disciple, who had reached the tomb first, also went inside. He saw and believed. (They still did not understand from Scripture that Jesus had to rise from the dead.)

Then the disciples went back to their homes, but Mary stood outside the tomb crying. As she wept, she bent over to look into the tomb and saw two angels in white, seated where Jesus' body had been, one at the head and the other at the foot.

They asked her, "Woman, why are you crying?"

"They have taken my Lord away," she said, "and I don't know where they have put him." At this, she turned around and saw Jesus standing there, but she did not realize that it was Jesus.

"Woman," he said, "why are you crying? Who is it you are looking for?"

Thinking he was the gardener, she said, "Sir, if you have carried him away, tell me where you have put him, and I will get him."

Jesus said to her, "Mary."

She turned toward him and cried out in Aramaic, "Rabboni!" (which means Teacher). Jesus said, "Do not hold on to me, for I have not yet returned to the Father. Go instead to my brothers and tell them, `I am returning to my Father and your Father, to my God and your God.' "

Mary Magdalene went to the disciples with the news: "I have seen the Lord!" And she told them that he had said these things to her.

On the evening of that first day of the week, when the disciples were together, with the doors locked for fear of the Jews, Jesus came and stood among them and said, "Peace be with you!" After he said this, he showed them his hands and side. The disciples were overjoyed when they saw the Lord.

Again Jesus said, "Peace be with you! As the Father has sent me, I am sending you." And with that he breathed on them and said, "Receive the Holy Spirit. If you forgive anyone his sins, they are forgiven; if you do not forgive them, they are not forgiven."

and

Luke 24 1-12

On the first day of the week, very early in the morning, the women took the spices they had prepared and went to the tomb. They found the stone rolled away from the tomb, but when they entered, they did not find the body of the Lord Jesus. While they were wondering about this, suddenly two men in clothes that gleamed like lightning stood beside them. In their fright the women bowed down with their faces to the ground, but the men said to them, "Why do you look for the living among the dead? He is not here; he has risen! Remember how he told you, while he was still with you in Galilee: `The Son of Man must be delivered into the hands of sinful men, be crucified and on the third day be raised again.' "Then they remembered his words.

When they came back from the tomb, they told all these things to the Eleven and to all the others. It was Mary Magdalene, Joanna,

Mary the mother of James, and the others with them who told this to the apostles. But they did not believe the women, because their words seemed to them like nonsense. Peter, however, got up and ran to the tomb. Bending over, he saw the strips of linen lying by themselves, and he went away, wondering to himself what had happened.

It's that time of year again. Easter! The day in the year when everyone celebrates ……Chocolate!! Chocolate eggs, chocolate bunnies, chocolate chickens, cream eggs, hollow eggs, eggs filled with all our favorite sweets, every possible variation from the white to the darkest, all celebrating Easter, even though chocolate wasn't actually around two thousand years ago. I also have to say I am not sure what eggs and bunnies etc. actually have to do with Easter. Of course I hear you say, it's all to do with new life, life out of dead appearing eggs and so on, but if we stop to think about it these are much more symbols of spring than of the resurrection of the Son of God. Also of course, unlike Christmas, the celebration of Easter is a movable feast, never on the same Sunday two years running. Strange isn't it that the most important event of the Christian year should be celebrated in a pagan way, on a Sunday which is fixed by the number of full moons after Christmas. Perhaps it is time to put the eggs down and start thinking a bit more about Easter.

The Anglican lectionary, which dictates the readings for each Sunday for a three year cycle, gives two gospel readings for this Sunday called Easter in 2015, one is the reading from John printed above; although I must admit I have added the last two verses, for reasons I will talk about later, A second service may use the reading from Luke. One I am sure we will all recognise, and one not so common; both differ in many of the details. In fact if we were to look at the four gospels, there are significant differences in the four accounts of the Easter story. Strange that this pivotal point of

Christianity should be the only part that the four gospel writers all appear to disagree with each other on. It also strongly reminds us that the gospel writers wrote down what they had heard, and reported it in their own style, a bit like newspaper reporters. They may witness the same event, but what appears in their individual newspapers will vary, and the gospels are not like the video news images or filmed reports that we are used to today, they need time to sit and ponder on, and to try and work out what was going on.

We all, of course, know the John reading well, and if we were asked to talk about Easter I expect it would be the one we talk about, but is it correct? If we look at the two readings for this Easter we see that in John's gospel Mary Magdalene goes alone to the tomb, whereas Luke says, "women" plural; also the women were carrying spices, suggesting they were going to complete the burial rituals that were started on the Friday, but would have had to stop on the Sabbath (Saturday, when no work was allowed) Only later does Luke mention that one of the women was Mary Magdalene. Mary does seem to be a key figure both at the foot of the cross and again here, it seems strange that such an important role is played by someone whom the church has deemed a prostitute. Perhaps a more open minded look at Mary of Magdala is needed when you have time!

Both readings then agree that the stone blocking the door had been removed, or rolled away. But the reactions of the women are very different. In John, Mary immediately turns and runs back to Peter and another disciple; whereas in Luke she entered the tomb and found it empty. Mary appears to be shocked and frightened by the rolled away stone; whereas in the second story the women almost appear to be expecting it. Perhaps they were worried at the time about the problem of how they were going to get into the tomb to complete the rituals. Instead two characters in clothes "gleaming like lightening" appear by the side of them, and they're afraid and bow down low.

Meanwhile in the other story Mary Magdalene has run back to Peter and the "disciple whom Jesus loved" making another profound appearance, but without being named. Who is he? Well I've got my ideas but this is not the place. The lads then run down to the tomb, Peter in the lead, overtaken by the other. This one arrives first, looks in, sees the grave cloths, but doesn't go in. Peter arrives, and true to the character we know from the gospels, in he goes. Then the other one follows, and both believe that the tomb is empty. Then the lads go home to have a good think. Mary stays, crying, totally distraught, but eventually she goes in and is faced by two men in white, quietly sitting where the body should have been. Mary isn't afraid, as the men obviously aren't flashing like the men in Luke's version, so she asks if they know where the body is. Then we assume she hears a noise behind her, because she turns and sees the gardener, who asks why she is crying. She tells him, and he simply says "Mary" and in this one word he is revealed to her.

 Her reply is simply "Rabonni" and this I find fascinating. If you ask anyone about Jesus' job, they will say he was a carpenter. How many times do the Gospel's say this? None! Was Jesus a Rabbi, everyone will say no, even though there are lots of times in the gospels that Jesus is referred to as Rabbi, or in this case Rabonni, the same word. If Jesus was not a Rabbi, why at this crucial first meeting with the risen Lord does Mary use this term of address, not his name, or Lord or anything else, just a simple use of the word Rabbi? Perhaps a time to stop and think about who you think Jesus was.

Then Jesus says

"Do not hold on to me, for I have not yet returned to the Father. Go instead to my brothers and tell them, `I am returning to my Father and your Father, to my God and your God.' "

Mary was obviously going to hug him, so he has to say no, then he tells her to go and tell the others "I am returning to my Father", clearly stating that He is the Son of God. But he goes on to say "Your Father", again clearly stating that we too are children of God, and why we too can address God as "Our Father" as we do every time we say the Lord's prayer. Again is this a good time to stop and think about those words "Your Father" and consider the awesome meaning of those words?

He continues then, saying that he is returning to his God and our God. This saying appears to contradict the teachings of the church as written in the fourth century in Nicea. The church teaches this peculiar Trinity of three in one and one in three, and says Jesus is God. Here Jesus claims neither. Jesus states he is returning to his God, which is tricky if he is already there with God, being God. Jesus claims to be the Son of God, NOT God, a thing which he has never claimed in the gospels, in fact has spent all his time pointing the way to God, and how we should live our lives to be able to take our turn in returning to our father God. Worshipping Jesus as God is not what he says he wants, and fights against it throughout the Gospels. This notion is the creation of Paul, who is the founder of the church, but does not always teach what Jesus teaches. If you think I'm wrong perhaps a comparative study of the gospels and letters may surprise!

Mary then returns to the men.

In Luke we find a very different story. The men in white give an explanation of what has happened but no sign of Jesus himself. The group of women return to the men who do not believe them, and only Peter himself goes to the tomb and finds it empty. End of story.

So back we go to John, where we find Mary returning to the others with a great shout of joy, "I have seen the Lord" and then telling them all about her adventure. The reading then stops. Even though there is more told of the Easter day events, and I think have a great impact on the meaning of the resurrection.

The account moves to the evening and they are all gathered in a locked room, frightened, confused and not really knowing what's going on. Very different to Luke where the men in white had explained it all. Jesus again appears and says "Peace be with you" and they are all overjoyed. Then he shows them his hands and side, and goes on.

Again Jesus said, "Peace be with you! As the Father has sent me, I am sending you." And with that he breathed on them and said, "Receive the Holy Spirit. If you forgive anyone his sins, they are forgiven; if you do not forgive them, they are not forgiven."

After a repeat of the peace, Jesus says that he was sending them out, and that means by inference that we are being sent out, to do his work. Also at this point Jesus breathes on them and fills them with the Holy Spirit, not at Pentecost, but as part of the Easter act. Then he makes the statement that if his followers forgive peoples sins, they are forgiven; and if they don't forgive, they are not forgiven. The power to forgive sins is not down to the act of love on the cross, but in the giving of the Holy Spirit as part of the resurrection gift. It is no wonder the church doesn't like these verses being said at Easter! The whole message of the forgiveness of sins changes from the cross to the resurrection and the power given to each of us by the Holy Spirit.

Are we surprised by this, I hope not, as each time we say the Lord's prayer we not only accept the Fathership of God, but we also say,

"Forgive us our trespasses (sins) as we forgive those who trespass (sin) against us." What we perhaps fail to grip is the importance of these words. We have the power to forgive, and be forgiven by each other, and perhaps it is this forgiveness that is the true message of Easter. "Father forgive them for they know not what they do" Words from the cross, Jesus has the power to forgive, but also asks his Father God to forgive them as well, a tough job in the situation, as any Father would say if he was watching His Son being killed. A great insight into the nature of Father and Son, even Godly ones. We have the same power of forgiveness given to us through the Holy Spirit.

But enough of my thoughts, although I hope by now you are starting to realize that when you study the gospels together, even just two of them, things are not as cut and dried as you first perhaps thought. So what are the key points to discuss?

13

I suppose the first thing to do is to consider is what do you think went on, you have two versions here, talk them through with each other, are the differences important or not?

Secondly this mysterious figure of Mary Magdalene, or Mary of Magdala, the second title has been given as some believe she was from the royal family of Magdala, and hence having equal status to the prince of the house of David. Others say she was a prostitute! She appears to be very important to Jesus, who do you think she is?

Lastly, if you follow this series through from Easter to Pentecost, you will discover that I often get infuriated by the selected readings for the set Sunday's. The reason is that they are always cut off, or start, with crucial parts missing. Often they will start with something like, "He replied to them"; who is he, what was the question, or something similar. Today a couple of verses were missed from the end of the Easter day events. But to my mind incredible verses! What do you make of them?

Two questions the first concerns the Holy Spirit, do you think it was given on Easter Day or Pentecost, or both?

Secondly who can forgive sins, can you?

The Second Sunday of Easter

Doubting Thomas revisited

John 29 v 19- 31

On the evening of that first day of the week, when the disciples were together, with the doors locked for fear of the Jews, Jesus came and stood among them and said, "Peace be with you!" After he said this, he showed them his hands and side. The disciples were overjoyed when they saw the Lord.

Again Jesus said, "Peace be with you! As the Father has sent me, I am sending you." And with that he breathed on them and said, "Receive the Holy Spirit. If you forgive anyone his sins, they are forgiven; if you do not forgive them, they are not forgiven."

Now Thomas (called Didymus), one of the Twelve, was not with the disciples when Jesus came. So the other disciples told him, "We have seen the Lord!"

But he said to them, "Unless I see the nail marks in his hands and put my finger where the nails were, and put my hand into his side, I will not believe it."

A week later his disciples were in the house again, and Thomas was with them. Though the doors were locked, Jesus came and stood among them and said, "Peace be with you!" Then he said to Thomas, "Put your finger here; see my hands. Reach out your hand and put it into my side. Stop doubting and believe."

Thomas said to him, "My Lord and my God!"

Then Jesus told him, "Because you have seen me, you have believed; blessed are those who have not seen and yet have believed."

Jesus did many other miraculous signs in the presence of his disciples, which are not recorded in this book. But these are written that you may believe that Jesus is the Christ, the Son of God, and that by believing you may have life in his name.

Easter 2, or the second Sunday of Eastertide, or Low Sunday, or Quasimodo Sunday, or Thomas Sunday or the Sunday of Divine mercy; probably the Sunday with more names than any other I can think of. The first title is obvious, Easter last Sunday, so this is Easter 2, likewise if we think of the period between Easter and Pentecost as the season of Eastertide, then this is the second Sunday. It also is often called Low Sunday, officially because it is a very ordinary Sunday after the big events of the Sunday before; but also more cynically because of the attendance. I don't know why, but after the great celebrations of Easter day, the following week nobody comes. Not just the extra visitors missing, but also a lot of the regulars. Strange!

If we look towards the Roman church, we find it sometimes called Thomas Sunday, because of the readings. It appears that it is also known as Quasimodo Sunday! No not after the hunchback, but the other way around. In the Old Roman service, in Latin, each year the Introit included the words "Quasi Modo geniti infants" (as just born children) and so it was nicknamed Quasimodo Sunday. Victor Hugo later came to write his famous story of an orphan growing up as the deformed bell ringer, the Hunchback of Notre Dame.The story tells of a child found on the Sunday after Easter, and hence is called, Quasimodo. The name has fallen into antiquity with the passing of the Roman services being in Latin, so today it has been renamed the Sunday of Divine Mercy.

But with all these titles, why does no one turn up. After the most amazing story of last week, why hasn't it inspired people to want to find out more about the event that changed the world? Or were they just there for the chocolate!! Let's take a look at the reading and see if there are any clues.

OK, the first couple of verses we have already thought about, for I really believe that if you are going to have the Easter day story, it should all be told on Easter day. The giving of the Holy Spirit to the followers and the power to forgive sins is all part of the resurrection package. It destroys the importance of the giving of the Holy Spirit and his part n the Easter message if left until the week after, as we have here. It makes the story more real if we stop and consider what it must have been like to not only find that Jesus was risen from the dead, but then for him to not only appear to you, but to empower you; The emotions must have been running at an all time high. Stop and imagine it, you spend three years of your life living and working with the Son of God. You see miracles, you see people being healed, you hear teachings of the most amazing wisdom and common sense at the same time; you are convinced he is the Messiah; but then he's dead! One Friday it all stops. Was he just another pretender, there were plenty around? But dead; and killed as a criminal, strung up between thieves. Where did it leave you? But then the Easter Day events and it culminates in a personal visit, not just some activity in the churchyard, but when you got together, frightened because you didn't understand what was going on, Jesus appears to you and fills you with the Holy Spirit. No wonder all you want to do is to talk about it. What it was like to see Jesus, what you felt when he filled you with his spirit,, and did the others feel the same?

Now imagine you're Thomas, and you weren't there. Like the others you had the same hopes and aspirations, the same shock when it all appeared to go wrong. And now all they are doing is going on about Jesus being alive and meeting them. How do you react? Stop for a while and think of yourself in the situation of Thomas. How would you feel? Jealous of them and this new joy they seem to have? Angry with yourself, because you missed it by not being there? Angry with people you were with, was it their fault you weren't there? Do you feel let down, hurt? Do you wish they would just shut up about it and realise how much it is hurting you to have it rubbed in that you weren't there. Is the only way for you to react is to shout "I DO NOT BELIEVE IT"

I often wonder why Thomas doubted, and the more I think of the situation, I think I probably would have done the same if it were me. As a science trained teacher for some thirty years I can hear myself asking for evidence; hard evidence; that Jesus is alive, and without evidence, no proof, no belief.

So the following Sunday they all get together again, and at last we are talking of events that are recorded as happening today, and Jesus again appears. His first words again "Peace be with you". Jesus knows of the turmoil within the group, the emotions, not only in Thomas, but perhaps in the others; was it real, was it a dream? But now Jesus has shown himself again, and his words calm the group. Thomas is then invited to get the proof he demanded, to put his hands onto Jesus' wounds. But Thomas doesn't need to, he sees and he believes, and simply says, "My Lord and my God". Jesus doesn't tell him off for his lack of faith, his need for proof, he accepts it, and just extends the message to include all who believe in his resurrection, even without seeing Him.

The book of John then closes. All that comes after this is added on later, maybe even a different author, we don't know. But the ending sums up the gospel

Jesus did many other miraculous signs in the presence of his disciples, which are not recorded in this book. But these are written that you may believe that Jesus is the Christ, the Son of God, and that by believing you may have life in his name.

The purpose of the Gospel is to tell you about the events of Jesus' life so that you may believe, and by believing you may have life. A wonderful conclusion to the Easter story, so why is there no one to hear it. What are we doing wrong as Christians, that the churches fill on Easter Sunday, but people don't return this week, for this is low Sunday. I remember in one church every window had a poster displayed in it declaring it was Holy Week. These were displayed during the week before Easter. On Easter day the message, "He is risen" was attached across the middle of every poster.

By this week they were taken down because Easter was over!!! The Anglican greeting for Easter tide, " Christ is risen", with the response "He is risen indeed" is now being mumbled by a few, while many have returned to "Peace be with you" said out of routine, with no enthusiasm. Easter is over, back to normal. Why?

Are we like Thomas, we hear of people being excited by the message of the risen Christ, enthusiastic about this final miracle, skeptical of the power of the Holy Spirit? Do we just go through the routine of Easter, try to make our services trendy to get more people in. The question has to be asked, that if people came on Easter day, for the greatest event in the history of the world, why haven't they returned?

The gospel message is simply believe in the fact that Jesus is the Son of God, he died and rose again, and in the gospels he gives us a pattern for our lives and then tells us to follow this pattern.. He gives us the power of the Holy Spirit and gives us life. Love God and love your neighbour, that's it!.

All the rest, big words and rules of how to believe and worship have been added by Paul and the churches over the years. Perhaps a simpler church, re examining what the gospels say, and following them with emotion, enthusiasm and conviction may do an awful lot of good in these troubled times.

So now some points to discuss if you didn't talk about things on the way through.

Firstly the person of Thomas, (often portrayed as a belligerent non believer), Thomas the "Doubter" as if that was all he did. Is this view upheld when you read this week's reading alone, or does it change when you put in the first two verses on Easter Day. I have shown my feelings above, do you agree? Also how would you have reacted if you were Thomas?

I suppose the second question has to reflect how we feel about Easter. Is it a one week event, or should it be dragged out until Pentecost. Does no one come back because the Easter Story wasn't retold with power, imagination, inspiration and excitement. Was it lost in the formality of the service. Is the feeling reflected in the fact that many clergy I have known go on holiday just after Easter, so no momentum is planned. If we spent hours planning special liturgy for the days, different hymns, no robes and other new ideas, did we get it right. (I remember being very trendy and using a guitar in Church, not giving a thought that to outsiders acoustic guitar music went out of fashion some twenty years earlier)

How do we tell the Easter story and inspire people?

The Third Sunday of Easter

Gone Fishing!

John 21   1-20

Afterward Jesus appeared again to his disciples, by the Sea of Tiberias. It happened this way: Simon Peter, Thomas (called Didymus), Nathanael from Cana in Galilee, the sons of Zebedee, and two other disciples were together. "I'm going out to fish," Simon Peter told them, and they said, "We'll go with you." So they went out and got into the boat, but that night they caught nothing.

Early in the morning, Jesus stood on the shore, but the disciples did not realize that it was Jesus. He called out to them, "Friends, haven't you any fish?" "No," they answered. He said, "Throw your net on the right side of the boat and you will find some." When they did, they were unable to haul the net in because of the large number of fish.

Then the disciple whom Jesus loved said to Peter, "It is the Lord!" As soon as Simon Peter heard him say, "It is the Lord," he wrapped his outer garment around him (for he had taken it off) and jumped into the water. The other disciples followed in the boat, towing the net full of fish, for they were not far from shore, about a hundred yards. Then they landed, they saw a fire of burning coals there with fish on it, and some bread.

Jesus said to them, "Bring some of the fish you have just caught." Simon Peter climbed aboard and dragged the net ashore. It was full of large fish, 153, but even with so many the net was not torn. Jesus said to them, "Come and have breakfast." None of the disciples dared ask him, "Who are you?" They knew it was the Lord. Jesus came, took the bread and gave it to them, and did the same with the fish. This was now the third time Jesus appeared to his disciples after he was raised from the dead.

When they had finished eating, Jesus said to Simon Peter, "Simon son of John, do you truly love me more than these?"

"Yes, Lord," he said, "you know that I love you."

Jesus said, "Feed my lambs."

Again Jesus said, "Simon son of John, do you truly love me?"

He answered, "Yes, Lord, you know that I love you."

Jesus said, "Take care of my sheep."

The third time he said to him, "Simon son of John, do you love me?"

Peter was hurt because Jesus asked him the third time, "Do you love me?" He said, "Lord, you know all things; you know that I love you."

Jesus said, "Feed my sheep. I tell you the truth, when you were younger you dressed yourself and went where you wanted; but when you are old you will stretch out your hands, and someone else will dress you and lead you where you do not want to go." Jesus said this to indicate the kind of death by which Peter would glorify God. Then he said to him, "Follow me!"

Easter 3, and another reading from John, even though it was clear last week that John's Gospel ended at the end of the last chapter. So who wrote this? Why and when? It is a mystery? But it is the set reading for this Sunday, so let's have another look at it, not just going for the obvious fishing bit, but to see if there is more we need to find in some of the details.

It appears to me to begin in a very normal way When I think, a crowd of men, who are not sure what's going on, and are not sure what to do, they often return to something they feel secure in, usually their work. For Peter and the others they are very confused about Jesus. They had supper with him, then he was arrested; then tried and sentenced to death. They watched him die on the cross ,but then the risen Lord appears; and then disappears again; is he dead or alive? So many questions unsolved in their minds. So what do a crowd of fisherman do? Go fishing! And not surprisingly, when your minds not on it, it doesn't work.! All night they work, but no fish! How often do we sit and try do something when our hearts not really in it and our mind is elsewhere; and we find it all goes wrong? I know it happens to me a lot. But then a stranger on the shore asks about their luck, and says to throw the net over the other side of the boat. The net fills, but doesn't break. Then a disciple knows who it is on the beach and yells "It is the Lord." Again we see this disciple named only as the disciple Jesus loved. Who is he, I have my ideas, but I will put them all together in a separate article for you to chew over, agree or disagree. But right now more important things are about to take place.

Peter has been feeling more down than the others, he remembers being told he would deny knowing Jesus three times, he remembers saying never; and then he remembers doing it. He remembers Mary Magdalene telling him that the tomb was empty, and shooting off, only to be overtaken by the others. So this is his big chance. He is a fisherman, used to water, swimming and moving through them, So over the side he goes and rushes to the shore, leaving the others to bring in fish and boat,

Peter and Jesus are obviously talking to each other as the boat arrives, so Jesus asks Peter to go and get some of the fish. Jesus then cooks breakfast and they all sit down to eat. Jesus, apart from the fish, also takes bread and gives it to them. The net filling, the giving of bread, memories of an earlier fishing trip, the giving of bread and the last supper, they know who is eating with them. This is then referred to as the third time Jesus appeared, twice behind locked doors, now on the beach. Is this a coincidence or is the author trying to make a significant point of the number 3, and things happening three times?

After breakfast Jesus and Peter have a quiet chat, and Peter is asked if he loves Jesus more than the other disciples. Peter replies that he does. Jesus responds in a very strange way, he says "Feed my lambs"

Jesus asks again "Do you truly love me?" the question digging deeper into Peter's guilty feelings. Peter again replies that Jesus knows that he loves him, and again a strange reply "Take care of my sheep"

Then Jesus asks a third time and Peter is getting upset, he's sorry about the denials, he's told Jesus that he loves him and now he's being asked again, so he replies to Jesus saying he knows everything, so he knows that he loves him; and Jesus again says something strange. "Feed my sheep".

Normally at this stage of a reflection, or a sermon, the preacher/author will start to talk of the significance of asking Peter three times about his love for Jesus. Three times balancing out the three denials. There is no doubt in my mind that this is probably true. The number three does seem to be important to John in his gospel, and whoever is adding this section is following the same style. But what of the three replies. Jesus' initial question is basically repeated three times, and Peter's reply is essentially the same each time. But these extra comments by Jesus are similar, and together they form a very clear progression of ideas for Peter to follow.

Feed my lambs.

Take care of my sheep.

Feed my sheep.

Remember at this stage back to a previous conversation; to the one where Simon had his name changed by Jesus and Simon became Peter, (Petros meaning stone or rock) and Jesus was saying that upon the rock of Peter he was going to build a church. Why Peter? Well he seems very ordinary, practical, down to earth sort of fisherman. He isn't perfect, and makes big mistakes, as the three denials before the trial prove. But he shows he is capable of genuine sorrow, and a real ambition to get it right next time. Overtaken in a race to the tomb, this time he wins the race. So I believe Jesus has forgiven his denials, and is now giving him instructions on church building.

No, not the sort of thing that springs to mind when we think about church buildings, Jesus has already told us that this is not what following him is

24

about, but that it's about people. Jesus, I believe, is saying that as news of the resurrection spreads people are going to be interested in what's going on. They will be nosey, hopeful, and many other things. Is Jesus the Son of God? Is Jesus the messiah? Has he really risen from the dead? When do they throw the Romans out of Israel? People interested, but lacking knowledge; coming to Christianity like new born lambs. Peter is told to feed them.

Peter is not a shepherd, but a fisherman, but he will know that if the food is wrong, the lamb dies. So he is being charged with gently feeding the newly interested followers with just the correct diet of experiences so that they too will love and follow Jesus. He is to watch them as they grow from lamb to sheep. And as they do he is to take care of the sheep. Not just the new converts, but the ones who have heard, believed, but then started to doubt, have second thoughts, found it not quite what they expected.

Peter is charged with helping them through this patch, and to continue to feed them, revealing more of the truth of the Risen Son of God. Not just quoting chunks of scripture but as a gentle growth pattern, not just putting them out to grass to feed themselves, but to feed them.

Isn't this what Jesus wanted for his church? As we read the gospels, isn't it Jesus' message to care for people when they want to get to know him, and follow him? Isn't it our responsibility, if we are part of the church Peter built, to follow his example? So let's ask ourselves seriously where we stand in our churches today. Do we ever go out into our communities, as Jesus instructed us to do, to show the love of God in action? Why should we? Because it is in response to our helping people that people will want to know why we are doing it. People will become lambs, and we should be ready to feed them. Not with great long sermons and lumps of bible quoted out of context, and especially not from the epistles with their complicated language, and ideas that contradict the gospel message, but a simple practical message that God loves them.

If people come to want to know more about Christianity, are our churches geared up to help people to move forward? Are there facilities to help with the growing problems of adjusting to a new and exciting faith? Or is it still just one service on a Sunday, doing as we are told, speaking only when allowed, sitting in rows looking at the back of people's heads, knowing people are behind us doing the same. The modern service is usually very unfriendly and as a result the people came at Easter but not the Sunday after, and by today, the crowds of two weeks ago are gone and forgotten. Nobody cared for the sheep.

Finally, for the ones who do remain, what opportunities are there for regular meetings, social groups, times to share and care! What chances to gather around the gospels and work out what they mean? Bible study is often so dull, where as it should be the most exciting. What did Jesus say and do? What did it mean to the people of the day, what does it mean to us?

Remember these three commands were given in response to Jesus asking Peter the same question he asks us, "Do you love me more than these?" If we are surrounded by friends in church the question is as pertinent today as two thousand years ago, and we need to answer honestly.

Jesus then gently let's Peter know how he will die. But notice again that the style of death will glorify, not Jesus, but God. Jesus the risen Son of God again pointing praise away from himself, and firmly toward his Father, God. Perhaps again we need to think whether our church worships God or Jesus, as Jesus appears to have no doubts?

Lots to think about and lots to reflect upon!

Firstly, if we call ourselves Christians, how do we answer Jesus when he asks us the question he asked Peter? When he asks if we love him more than these?

Secondly, how do we show that love to others so that they will want to share in it?

Thirdly Jesus clearly gives a three stage programme for learning about his ministry. What do our churches do to continue this pattern today? Jesus himself tells Peter about this, so it probably suggests that it works!

The Fourth Sunday of Easter

The Good Shepherd

John 10   22-30

Then came the Feast of Dedication at Jerusalem. It was winter, and Jesus was in the temple area walking in Solomon's Colonnade. The Jews gathered around him, saying, "How long will you keep us in suspense? If you are the Christ, tell us plainly."
Jesus answered, "I did tell you, but you do not believe. The miracles I do in my Father's name speak for me, but you do not believe because you are not my sheep. My sheep listen to my voice; I know them, and they follow me. I give them eternal life, and they shall never perish; no one can snatch them out of my hand. My Father, who has given them to me, is greater than all; no one can snatch them out of my Father's hand. I and the Father are one."

Here we are on the 4th Sunday after Easter, but suddenly the readings change back to way before the Easter events. Instead of resurrection appearances we find Jesus walking through the temple in the middle of winter and the crowds questioning him. One simple question in particular; in plain words, are you the Christ? A simple question, from a quiet, interested crowd who have gathered to talk.

It might just be me, but I find the lectionary annoying. The reason being my first question is to ask myself why they are asking this at this particular point in time? In what context are they asking? And why? This little reading means nothing out of context, or even worse, could be used to say things which aren't quite what Jesus meant. So we need to look at what went before, and see what Jesus is talking about. So let's go back a bit in John chapter 10 and start to put the reading in context.

28

"I am the good shepherd; I know my sheep and my sheep know me-- just as the Father knows me and I know the Father--and I lay down my life for the sheep. I have other sheep that are not of this sheep pen. I must bring them also. They too will listen to my voice, and there shall be one flock and one shepherd. The reason my Father loves me is that I lay down my life--only to take it up again. No one takes it from me, but I lay it down of my own accord. I have authority to lay it down and authority to take it up again. This command I received from my Father."

At these words the Jews were divided. Many of them said, "*He is demon-possessed and raving mad. Why listen to him*?" But others said, "*These are not the sayings of a man possessed by a demon. Can a demon open the eyes of the blind*?"

So we see Jesus referring to himself as the good shepherd. There were many good shepherds who not only knew their sheep, but were willing to lay down their lives for them. But Jesus goes on to say that he knows his Father and the Father knows him, and that the reason his Father loves him is that he is not only willing to lay down his life voluntarily for his sheep, but also has the power to take it up again. Jesus actually says he has the "Authority" to die and then rise again, a clear reference to the Easter events.

Jesus also says that apart from his followers, his own present sheep, he has others that will respond to him, and he will form one flock with one shepherd.

Jesus constantly refers to his Father, God, and hence is referring to himself as the Son of God. If this happened today in our churches how would we react? Probably much the same as the crowd who said, "He is raving mad, why listen to him." But others point to the miracles and are not so sure.

So now we know the reason behind the question, are you the Christ, or are you mad? And Jesus replies that he did tell them, perhaps not in so many words but in the miracles that they have seen him do in his Father's name.

They don't believe because they are not his sheep. He tells them that his sheep know him, know his voice, follow him, and in return he gives them eternal life. He clearly states that they "Will never perish", and no one can ever take them away from his Father's care. The final statement of the days reading "I and the Father are one"

The voice of authority states that he and God are one, and he has the power to grant eternal life; and so on that dramatic note one assumes that they all believe, and go on their way rejoicing, for the reading stops there! Sounds good, but it's not quite true. Here again we have to add to the reading another ten verses or so to get the end of the story. Here they are

Again the Jews picked up stones to stone him, but Jesus said to them, "I have shown you many great miracles from the Father. For which of these do you stone me?"
"We are not stoning you for any of these," replied the Jews, "but for blasphemy, because you, a mere man, claim to be God."
Jesus answered them, "Is it not written in your Law, `I have said you are gods'? If he called them `gods,' to whom the word of God came--and the Scripture cannot be broken-- what about the one whom the Father set apart as his very own and sent into the world? Why then do you accuse me of blasphemy because I said, `I am God's Son'? Do not believe me unless I do what my Father does. But if I do it, even though you do not believe me, believe the miracles, that you may know and understand that the Father is in me, and I in the Father."

No not quite the end today's reading infers. After the grandiose statement' they picked up their stones to carry on where they left off. Jesus, however, asks which particular miracle it is that he is being stoned for. The crowd replies that it's not for the miracles, but for blasphemy; for claiming to be God. Jesus then answers by quoting from Psalm 82, where the Psalm writer refers to people as gods. His argument then goes on to say that if God gives the psalmist His words, and they become "Scripture", then scripture can't be untrue. On those grounds Jesus can claim to be the Son of God. But he goes one further and claims not to be a Son of God, but

"The special Son of God," that is referred to in the scriptures, and hence his Father can perform miracles through him. The miracles show that Jesus is in the Father just as the father is in him.

Phew, a simple few verses, but when the context is added the whole great debate of the Trinity and what it is comes into play. For here Jesus says he is the Son of God, but that he and the Father are one, He also quotes back to the psalms, and the one he quotes starts off by saying,

"God has taken His place in the divine council, In the midst of the gods he will hold judgement."

So now we have a real problem, we are taught by the church that there is only one God, but here we find God taking his place amongst a council of gods. Well it's obviously wrong, and anyway the Old Testament isn't meant to be taken literally, is it? If we quote the Bible we always make sure we quote Jesus. But here it is Jesus not only quoting scripture, but saying that scripture can't be broken. If we start to pick and choose which bits we believe in the gospels we are really making up our own convenient religion. There are lots of references to other God's, and even today while many church goers will stand and say "I believe in one God" by the time they get home and put on the news, not many say that Allah does not exist.

Jesus is the Son of God, and God is his Father, they are a very close family, but I do not believe that they are literally one. Of one mind, yes; of one spirit yes; of one being, (can anyone one tell me what that means) probably not. Jesus does all in his father's name, for the glory of his Father, not for himself, how can they be the same? And this is before we add the Holy Spirit into the equation!

A very short reading, out of context meaning one thing, in context something else, so where do we start with our discussions. As usual these ideas are only suggestions, you might already be deep in discussion, but if not, try these.

Firstly if someone came to your church and started to talk as Jesus did, how would your church react. Would you think him mad, or bad or God, to use an Alpha course phrase. Henri Nouwen, in one of his books writes out an application form to train as a priest. The person applying is called Mr. E Mannuel. He wasn't accepted.

Secondly, let's consider this knotty problem of the idea of the Trinity. The Nicene Creed says we believe. or the Apostles Creed says I believe, in One God. Is this what Jesus is saying here? If we only believe that there is one God, what about Allah, Krishna, and the many others worshipped throughout the world today? Not to mention all those of Greece, Egypt and the Old Testament. If there is only one God, is Jesus a God, even though he never claims to be. If the Father is God, and Jesus is the son of God, and Mary is the Mother of Jesus, is Mary a God. OK, I won't go on, but we have to be sure of what we believe. Do we believe that there is only one God, if so which one; or do we believe that the best God is the creator of the world, the God, whose son is Jesus?

The fifth Sunday of Easter

A New Commandment

John13 31-35

When he was gone, Jesus said, "Now is the Son of Man glorified and God is glorified in him. If God is glorified in him, God will glorify the Son in himself, and will glorify him at once.
"My children, I will be with you only a little longer. You will look for me, and just as I told the Jews, so I tell you now: Where I am going, you cannot come.
"A new command I give you: Love one another. As I have loved you, so you must love one another. By this all men will know that you are my disciples, if you love one another."

It's done it again! What a way to start a gospel reading that is supposed to teach us about the life and works of Jesus. "When he was gone"! Well where was he? Where is he going? When is this happening? Why can't the lectionary put things into context? OK, so this is the fifth Sunday after Easter, so it must be something to do with a resurrection story, mustn't it? Yes? No!!!

The reading actually comes at the end of John's account of the last supper. The bread and wine have been taken and the feet have been washed. Judas has just left to go and betray Jesus. The others are going out to take part in the final acts before the arrest on the Thursday before Easter, Jesus knows what's going to happen but it's complicated.

Jesus again refers to himself as the "Son of man" not the "Son of God", as what he is about to face is for the human race. His ministry will reach its climax at the resurrection. But firstly, in the act on the cross Jesus will be glorified, and God in Him will be glorified. The reason being that if God glorifies himself in Jesus, then Jesus must by default be glorified. This is not going to be a slow process but will happen at once.

If we stop and think about it, Jesus has spent his entire ministry turning aside from personal glorification, but pointing his finger to his Father who makes all things happen. Suddenly, though,, this act upon the cross, it would appear, can only happen if the Son of Man is seen as the Son of God. So God must glorify both. At least that's how I see it, what do you make of it?

Jesus then tells them he is going where they cannot go. To his death!

Then comes the easy bit, the new commandment, to love one another.

Let's just stop and think for a moment. This is not a new idea, or a new suggestion, or a new recommendation; it's a command. From this position on the eve of his death, Jesus orders those present, and us, us to love one another. Why? Because it is by this that all people will know that we are his followers. It's not a new idea, Jesus, in the summary of the law, tells us to love our neighbours as ourselves, and in my lent course two sessions are spent on discussing loving our neighbour, and loving ourselves. So when we put the two versions of the same commandment together, we see that our neighbours in fact become everybody, in neighbouring houses, streets, towns, counties, countries; and one day maybe even worlds!

Likewise when we looked at how we should love ourselves, it was not in a selfish egocentric way, but enough to realize we have talents that are unique, and finding enough time to use those skills for God.

So we see that love for one another does not just become something to be shared around amongst a small group of friends, who then become in danger of becoming a clique; but becomes again loving and caring for everyone.

I put on the 'Facebook' page a few weeks ago, about a poor, unkempt, dirty smelly lady who wanted to be baptized and become a church member. The vicar twice told her to go away and pray about it, just to "make sure" it was right. He didn't want her in his church. She didn't return. The punch line comes when he bumps into her some time later and asks if she had prayed again, and what had God told her. She said she had prayed and God had told her not to worry, he couldn't get into that church either.

A silly story perhaps, but certainly has a ring of truth. When we think of loving one another do we actually stop and think that some of the others may not be like us. They could be richer; or poorer. They could be humble, or self-opinionated loud mouths. They could be much better dressed, better spoken; or they could be down and out. They could be a different colour, or a different creed, and in this present war torn world how easy is it to love people who are killing others. Would we welcome any of these into our churches? But if we can't, are we showing that we are good disciples.

It's not easy; easy to say perhaps, but not easy to do.

The reading goes on with the section that Peter says he would happily lay down his life for Jesus, and is told he will deny him three times. But Peter kept on trying and look what he did for Jesus after his ressurection.

If we cannot be open to everybody, not just our friends and our fellow church goers, then the church can become an inward looking tight clique. No love here!

When new people come to your church for the first time, talk to them, get them coffee, ask them around for dinner, be nice to them. You never know, they might even come back a second week,

Why not try something really exciting! Perhaps there are ways that as Christians we could move out from our churches and love people in our community. Befriend them, help them, just talk to the lonely, and perhaps just love them!

This is perhaps a good time to stop and think about how we can show our love for others outside of our church and work communities. We are commanded to love each other, it is not an option but how can we do it in the modern world when we are so busy. The question must be asked "are we too busy for God"?

If we remember back a couple of weeks Jesus gave Peter instructions for a three part plan to essentially "love people into the Kingdom of God", a wonderful phrase that I picked up many years ago. How can we, and our churches love people to God.

Are we trying to love people into loving God, or filling our churches? The two are not necessarily the same.

Sixth Sunday of Easter

If any loves me he will obey my teaching

John 14 23-29

Jesus replied, "If anyone loves me, he will obey my teaching. My Father will love him, and we will come to him and make our home with him. He who does not love me will not obey my teaching. These words you hear are not my own; they belong to the Father who sent me.

"All this I have spoken while still with you. But the Counselor, the Holy Spirit, whom the Father will send in my name, will teach you all things and will remind you of everything I have said to you. Peace I leave with you; my peace I give you. I do not give to you as the world gives. Do not let your hearts be troubled and do not be afraid.

"You heard me say, `I am going away and I am coming back to you.' If you loved me, you would be glad that I am going to the Father, for the Father is greater than I. I have told you now before it happens, so that when it does happen you will believe

I think by now you know what I am going to say; in between the screams of frustration! How on earth is anyone supposed to learn the meaning of the words of the gospel when the readings are chosen starting with comments like "Jesus replied" How on earth can we study an answer when we don't know the question? Or who he's talking to? Or what is the context of the discussion? I am sorry for my outburst, but it seems to me that every reading set aside for the Easter season has been taken out of context, and trimmed to try and prove a point, that as we have discovered does not always reflect the full meaning of the events. So let us once again look at what went before, and after, and see what it says.

The reading is taken again from John's account of the last supper. The bread and wine have been taken and shared; Jesus has washed the feet of those gathered, and now Jesus is talking about the immediate future of his death and resurrection. He also talks of the coming of the Holy Spirit. He has told the disciples to love one another, to trust in him and he will be with them. He has just been talking about revealing himself to the disciples, but not the whole world. It is Judas, but specifically not Judas Iscariot, who asks Jesus how will he reveal himself to just his followers. It is to this question that Jesus replies as above.

The first thing he says is that anyone who loves him will obey his teaching. This would appear obvious at first, but when I stop to consider this comment I ask myself whether I actually know the teachings of Jesus. The answer I came to a few years ago was that I probably didn't. I knew the teachings of the church, much of which is based upon Paul's teaching; and the more I looked I realized that the gospels appear to give a different view from those of the letters of Paul.. The end result of this train of thought has led eventually to this series of Bible studies; and also the website on which I put up these weekly reflections on what I think they mean. But they are always open to discussion and you may not agree with my thoughts, but I ask you to at least think of what Jesus says. It appears to me to be worth it, for if we love Jesus and obey his teachings, both God and Jesus will be with us, and that's what I think being a Christian is all about.

But what of those who don't love, Jesus says simply that they won't obey. The result is left open, but there is a strong inference that if we don't obey, then we can't claim to love! But these words do not just belong to Jesus, but come direct from his father, God. It's not just a case of trying to learn teachings and remember them, but to follow them., Jesus then promises us that after he has gone to the Father, if we love him, he will send the Holy Spirit to remind us of Jesus and teach us more about his ways. So we are not to worry about it.

Peace I leave with you; my peace I give you. I do not give to you as the world gives. Do not let your hearts be troubled and do not be afraid.

Jesus gives us his peace, and promises it will stay with us, as long as we love and obey. The peace of God, which Jesus tells us is not an uncertain peace as we experience when we hear of peace talks and ceasefires on the evening news, but a peace which says we do not have to be troubled or worry, we haven't got to be afraid of consequences. The peace which God promises means that we can totally trust and rely on God to be with us in all that we do.

I wonder how many times we hear the word peace in church on a Sunday, when we pray for peace between countries, beliefs, tribes and any other group of people who appear to not be able to live next door to each other without dreams of power, and the resulting bloodshed that this always brings. This is a good thing to do, but it is not the peace of God. That's the thing that gets a quick mention right at the end of the service when the Vicar's moving off to get first in the coffee queue.

"The peace of God, which passes all understanding, keep your hearts and minds in Jesus Christ. Amen"

Words said every Sunday, and quoted directly from the book of common Worship, but do they mean anything to us? To say the peace of God passes all understanding appears to me to be a great cop out! Why? This reading tells us clearly that if we truly come to rely on His spirit within us then we do not need to worry, or be troubled or afraid. God is with us, he loves us, will care for us; and it is in that knowledge we can be at total peace. Is it easy? No, of course not, but surely the message of the gospels is to keep on trying to love and obey. When you get it wrong, admit it, be sorry and start over again, we have to work towards God's peace, but it isn't a once in a lifetime chance, like peace in the world, shattered when someone fires the first bullet in the ceasefire; but this is a personal internal peace with God from God.

Jesus then explains that he is going away to the Father, and that they should be pleased for him because he is going home to his Father, and then returning to them. Jesus is preparing them for the Easter events and there it ends, but it shouldn't! The Gospel has two more verses before this dialogue closes. I wonder why they were missed. Let's look at them

I will not speak with you much longer, for the prince of this world is coming. He has no hold on me, but the world must learn that I love the Father and that I do exactly what my Father has commanded me.

The last two verses before they go out from the upper room. "I will not speak with you much longer for the prince of this world is coming. He has no hold on me." Or as the New Revised Standard Version of the bible puts it

"I will no longer talk much with you, for the ruler of this world is coming, he has no power over me, but I do as the Father has commanded me so that the world may know that I love the Father"

Why is Jesus not going to talk much longer, the answer there must be the fact that he is going to his death, voluntarily. Why is this so important? Because the ruler of this world, the prince of this world, is coming to take up his post.. He has no power over Jesus he cannot make Jesus go to his death, Jesus gives himself voluntarily. So who is this prince of the world who is coming to rule the world? Jesus must be referring to some supernatural spirit or "Devil"

It is because of this ruler that we have to know the teachings of Jesus, so that we can obey them, and show that we love the one true creator God and his Son. The present ruler of the world is not God or Jesus, said by Jesus himself. This appears to be at odds with all the church teaches. If

Jesus is to have the "Victory over sin and death" as the churches claim, why does Jesus mention the coming ruler at this time?

I think Jesus is telling the truth, and that the world is not ruled by him at this present time. The ruler appears to like war, famine, destruction, hurt, in fact anything except love. Which is why we are being told here to obey the teachings of Jesus, and in doing so we must show love towards the Father, and one another. But as I started this reflection if we do not know what Jesus teaches, how can we show his love. Without loving and obeying we cannot be given the Holy Spirit, and we cannot find that elusive peace of God

Many do not believe this, do not love, follow other views, and it would appear to me, follow the present ruler of this earth. But, Jesus offers his peace when invited to do so, to each one of us.

A different view from that which the lectionary writers intended, but I feel a much more important understanding of what Jesus was saying. I Hope a study of this week's reading, with the extra two verses has made you think. Again it appears to me to alter the usual idea and purpose of the Easter events. At this stage I normally set some items to discuss, but today you may not need them. But just in case start by discussing whether you know the teachings of Jesus as written in the Bible, or in truth, do you just know the odd bit from Sunday School, church or where ever.

This study is based upon the reading from John's Gospel, I have never heard the ideas here preached in a church, although I have been told that evil doesn't exist, and the Holy Spirit would have to be controlled if he started stirring things up. Is the Church correct, or is Jesus?

The inference made by Jesus is that if you do not obey his teachings you cannot love him, is my understanding of this correct?

The seventh Sunday of Easter

Jesus Prays for us

John 17 20-26

"My prayer is not for them alone. I pray also for those who will believe in me through their message, that all of them may be one, Father, just as you are in me and I am in you. May they also be in us so that the world may believe that you have sent me. I have given them the glory that you gave me, that they may be one as we are one: I in them and you in me. May they be brought to complete unity to let the world know that you sent me and have loved them even as you have loved me.

"Father, I want those you have given me to be with me where I am, and to see my glory, the glory you have given me because you loved me before the creation of the world.

"Righteous Father, though the world does not know you, I know you, and they know that you have sent me. I have made you known to them, and will continue to make you known in order that the love you have for me may be in them and that I myself may be in them."

The last Sunday of the season called Easter tide and almost the last of the readings from John's gospel. Most of us will have passed by last Thursday without giving a thought to the remembrance of Jesus ascending back to heaven and his Father. Once a Bank Holiday, now a day when most give no thought to church or religion, despite its importance. If it needed celebrating perhaps it should have happened on a Sunday, when we have proper services! Still, enough of my ramblings, what do we make of this last Sunday reading before Pentecost? As usual it gives no clue as to context, so reading it alone we have difficulty understanding it. Also the opening is a bit like, not so much a "who's who", but more like a "who's in who". OK, let's start to look at it.

The setting is again the Thursday before Easter, the last supper is over and Jesus and his disciples are in the garden. They have talked, but now Jesus prays to his Father, just before the arrest and trial. The prayer though is made not only for the disciples present, but also for us;

" I pray also for those who will believe in me through their message, that all of them may be one, "

The disciples have their message and are charged to pass it on, we are charged to hear the message, believe it and act upon it, and as a result be united as one. I wonder where we went wrong? If we look at the various types of "Christians" today all in disagreement with one another over points of doctrine and truth we see that the splits and factions in the churches appear to come not from the teachings of Jesus, but dare I say, from the teachings of Paul, who, when we examine what Jesus says, appears to ignore the message of the Gospels. This may need much further study and discussion, but enough to mention it at this point.

Then the strange section about who is in whom, but perhaps it is easier to think of it as being of one spirit. United as one soul; each being part of a whole, but each part definitely separate, like being in one godly family, with God the creator as Father, and then Jesus his son. From what we read in the gospels, the miracles and the teachings, we can clearly see that Jesus is the Son of God, and that he does what he does because his father sent him and empowered him. Perhaps it is true that the churches, in concentrating on the cross so much, miss the importance of his life, for it is his life that reveals the truth. Remember, Jesus always says "I am" not "I will be".

It continues with the comment that it is by the glory of God, being seen through the life of Christ, and the actions of his followers, that allows God's glory to be seen in his followers, and as a result, unity!

"Father, I want those you have given me to be with me where I am, and to see my glory, the glory you have given me because you loved me before the creation of the world.

Jesus asks for his followers, and that includes us, to be allowed to be with Jesus and to see him in glory, able to see the love of God shown through his son. The prayer is a simple request, and appears to be at variance with much of the teaching of the church. No mention of the death and resurrection being needed to be believed in order to have sins forgiven, instead to be a part of God's family as a result of a prayer. If we remember on Easter day, we discovered that Jesus said **we** had the power to forgive sins. This we remind ourselves is true each time we use the Lord's Prayer and say "Forgive us our sins (trespasses) as we forgive those who sin (trespass) against us. This was the way the Lord's Prayer was written in the Alternate Service Book (ASB) for the church of England. It caused uproar, mainly because the words had been changed, but also because of the belief that sin can only be forgiven by God; (although he does appear to be able to do this acting through an ordained clergy person). Does this idea follow more from the way the church has used the forgiveness and sin, and the constant emphasis on sin and hell, to gain control of people over the years, rather than the words of the gospel?

This section again ends, as John's gospel starts, with the fact that Jesus and his Father were there before the world was created, and, therefore, by inference, Jesus' Father is the God who created the world, and not the prince who rules it at present who we discovered last week.

Righteous Father, though the world does not know you,

Read that through again, does it say what I think it says? Does it say that the world doesn't know the creator God that Jesus calls Father. Surely this must be wrong, for we all know there is only one God, don't we. The Jews were the chosen race, the Old Testament is the history of the relationship between God and Jew, so Jesus has obviously got this wrong, or it's a mistranslation. Or is it! Does the action of Jesus' father match the actions of the Old Testament God, the one who punishes the children of those who don't obey the Ten Commandments; The one who lies when he says Adam and Eve will die if they eat the apple, but they don't; The one who makes a hero of Moses, a murderer, and David, another murderer, remember he had a man killed because he fancied his wife, and so on.

How many times today do we really struggle with what God allows to happen today in the world, wars, famines, earthquakes, and more personally with sickness and death; all the problems of poverty and corruption. Does the world know God? Remember Jesus himself spoke of a ruler over whom he had no influence?

Near where I live a section of the population lived by the message of John's Gospel alone. As such they were peaceful, poor people, owning nothing, sharing all. They believed that the present earth was ruled by an evil God, and it was their job to ensure that they followed the teachings of Jesus and not the Ways of the world and thus gained salvation. The church called them heretics, introduced the inquisition and had them burnt at the stake. In fact a full scale crusade was launched against them. I ask, who were the ones who followed the creator God, and who the evil destroyer?

The creator God and his son are known by love, and shown by love. That love should be in us, Is it? Is it shown to others by us?

This is the last Sunday in Easter tide, and the reflections on this year's readings have uncovered some challenging thoughts, especially these kept for the last week. Jesus is remembered as returning to his Father last Thursday, he has told us the world is ruled not by him, but another. Jesus has promised to return, perhaps we should end this Easter tide with the prayer
"Amen, come Lord Jesus come"
Or perhaps, as a friend once put it,, at the time of a TV programme, "The price is right

"Come on down Lord Jesus, Come on down"!

Is this what we want? As the Easter series comes towards the Pentecost event we must ask ourselves if we really believe Jesus is going to return and then become the ruler of this world. Notice I only ask if you believe he will, not details of how it could be achieved.

Jesus asks that his message and teachings should be passed on by those who love him. How are you following this part of his message?

Can you forgive sins, you discussed this in the first week, do you still believe the same as you did then, or have your views changed?

Pentecost Sunday

Reflections on the Pentecost Gospel

John 14 8-17

Philip said, "Lord, show us the Father and that will be enough for us."

Jesus answered: "Don't you know me, Philip, even after I have been among you such a long time? Anyone who has seen me has seen the Father. How can you say, `Show us the Father'? Don't you believe that I am in the Father, and that the Father is in me? The words I say to you are not just my own. Rather, it is the Father, living in me, who is doing his work. Believe me when I say that I am in the Father and the Father is in me; or at least believe on the evidence of the miracles themselves. I tell you the truth, anyone who has faith in me will do what I have been doing. He will do even greater things than these, because I am going to the Father. And I will do whatever you ask in my name, so that the Son may bring glory to the Father. You may ask me for anything in my name, and I will do it.

"If you love me, you will obey what I command. And I will ask the Father, and he will give you another Counselor to be with you forever-- the Spirit of truth. The world cannot accept him, because it neither sees him nor knows him. But you know him, for he lives with you and will be in you.

OK, by now you will know what I am going to say, how can we understand and learn if we do not know the context in which the reading is set! A reading like this, with so many points to consider, rattled off. Of course in an Anglican service you have had to stand up, say or sing a few words, the vicar may have whooshed some incense over the book he is to read from, and yet somehow we are expected to understand this reading.

Of course this is the weekend of Pentecost, it used to be Whitsun, or White Sunday, the day of baptisms, but in Britain it may or may not coincide with the Spring bank Holiday. Interesting that Britain has Bank Holy Days, perhaps a new God is being worshipped!

I digress; this reading again from the last supper. Peter's forthcoming denial has been talked about, and Jesus has said that he is returning to his Father. He has told them his house has many rooms, the reading well known from funeral services. Phillip has asked how they will know the way to heaven, and Jesus has answered him. But Philip is still confused and unsure, so he asks Jesus to show him his Father. I don't quite know how he expected Jesus to do this, so Jesus gives his reply,

"Don't you know me, Philip, even after I have been among you such a long time? Anyone who has seen me has seen the Father. How can you say, `Show us the Father'? Don't you believe that I am in the Father, and that the Father is in me?"

Do I detect a touch of sadness, or is it exasperation in this reply. We cannot tell from the written word how the words were said, but Jesus is sad that even after a long time together the doubts are still there in his follower's minds. Again this reply that anyone who has seen Jesus has seen his Father, because they are together as one, working together with the Fathers power working through his son. Finally, almost in desperation Jesus tells Phillip, if you don't believe my words, at least open your eyes and see what I've done, let the miracles speak for themselves.

OK, so far we have seen this debate and struggles going on throughout the evening of the last supper and we know from Thomas they will continue after the resurrection. But the next bit is worrying for us as believers.

I tell you the truth, anyone who has faith in me will do what I have been doing. He will do even greater things than these, because I am going to the Father

Firstly Jesus confirms that what he is telling us is the truth, I say us because this speech is aimed not just at Phillip, but to anyone who loves God and has faith in him. Jesus then says that we will be able to do not just what Jesus was able to do, but even greater things. That needs a lot of thought on our part. Do we believe that we are able to do the things that Jesus could do. If not are we saying he was lying, or our faith isn't strong enough? Let's move on.

And I will do whatever you ask in my name, so that the Son may bring glory to the Father. You may ask me for anything in my name, and I will do it.

Jesus says, in truth, he will do whatever we ask in his name, in order to bring glory to his Father. If we ask in his name he will do it, not might, or maybe, or anything else, Jesus states he will do it. Wow, a quick trip to buy some lottery tickets seems in order, I will win, and a new house, a new car, a better job, wow, Jesus has said that if I ask he will do it. At last a free meal ticket. Is this what he means? I would suggest probably both yes and no. No, am I suggesting that Jesus is lying? The answer to that is definitely no!

How can it be both? Well, if I win the lottery am I likely to stand up and tell the world that Jesus won for me to gain his Father praise and glory. No! If I turn up at church, or work, with a new car, am I likely to give God the glory? No! If I ask for healing on a young child, and believe he will do it? Yes! The problem is in what we ask for and why we ask it. Jesus goes *on*

"If you love me, you will obey what I command"

Ah, the sting in the tail, the real hub of the debate, do I really love the Father, do I really love Jesus? If I do will my priorities be a new car, a new job with more money, a bigger house, a million pounds; or will my priorities be helping others to find their way into the Kingdom of heaven.

For this is what Jesus asks of us, to love God the Father, and our neighbours as ourselves, and be willing to do whatever is needed to let this happen. To help us he will send us help in the form of the Holy Spirit, to be in us, and guide us. The Spirit of truth! But it won't make for an easier life, because of the last part of this reading

the Spirit of truth. The world cannot accept him, because it neither sees him nor knows him. But you know him, for he lives with you and will be in you

The world cannot accept the spirit of truth, it can't see him, and it won't know him. The world at present appears to be about power, and riches. Those who rule do not really seem to care about the poor of the world, the sick, the starving the refugee. Politicians spend fortunes on election campaigns, and then make cuts in services because there is no money. Refugees are turned away from one country, while another struggles to save those risking their lives to escape war and torture. Listening to election campaign speeches from all parties the spirit of "Truth" does appear to be unknown, and unacceptable. Alas even the church appears to have lost its way with loving. Buildings and heating systems, and general repairs to the roof and tower appear to be more important than people.

But if you love the Father, the spirit of truth will be in you, and live with you, even though you may find life difficult, Jesus will in those cases hear your prayer and grant your wishes.

This is Pentecost, and the usual reading which everyone knows is the winds and flames retold in acts. Often quoted, but rarely believed. This series of reflections are based upon what Jesus said, of himself, his father and the spirit of truth. Many of the ideas do not appear to agree with what the church of today seems to say and do. I Started with a sarcastic comment but I hope you can know see why; I ask you seriously whether this year you are celebrating a Pentecost Holyday, or a Bank Holiday?

Once more the thrust of the reading is that in order to Love we have to follow the Teachings of God, as told by Jesus. If we do not know the teachings of Jesus, how can we follow them? If we cannot follow them how can we gain the help of the Holy Spirit? Without the Holy Spirit how can we pass on the love of God to others?

I leave you to discuss and decide!

Made in United States
Troutdale, OR
04/14/2025